Dumbass to Kickass

uncensored & unfiltered

Farah Naaz

Chennai • Bangalore

CLEVER FOX PUBLISHING
Chennai, India

Published by CLEVER FOX PUBLISHING 2024
Copyright © Farah naaz 2024

All Rights Reserved.
ISBN: 978-93-67075-43-2

This book has been published with all reasonable efforts taken to make the material error-free after the consent of the author. No part of this book shall be used, reproduced in any manner whatsoever without written permission from the author, except in the case of brief quotations embodied in critical articles and reviews.

The Author of this book is solely responsible and liable for its content including but not limited to the views, representations, descriptions, statements, information, opinions and references ["Content"]. The Content of this book shall not constitute or be construed or deemed to reflect the opinion or expression of the Publisher or Editor. Neither the Publisher nor Editor endorse or approve the Content of this book or guarantee the reliability, accuracy or completeness of the Content published herein and do not make any representations or warranties of any kind, express or implied, including but not limited to the implied warranties of merchantability, fitness for a particular purpose. The Publisher and Editor shall not be liable whatsoever for any errors, omissions, whether such errors or omissions result from negligence, accident, or any other cause or claims for loss or damages of any kind, including without limitation, indirect or consequential loss or damage arising out of use, inability to use, or about the reliability, accuracy or sufficiency of the information contained in this book.

TRIBUTE TO MY MENTORS AND EDUCATORS

I would like to extend my heartfelt gratitude to **Ibn Al Hytham Islamic School** and everyone who has played a significant role in my journey. Your unwavering support and dedication have made a profound impact on my life. Special thanks to the management, the teachers, the receptionist, the cashier, and everyone else who has always supported me and never let me give up. You all describe the true spirit of education. You have not only imparted academic knowledge but have also instilled moral values and nurtured the inner soul of every student.

I am especially grateful to my IP teacher - Mrs. Aakhila; Accounts teacher - Mrs. Anila; head teacher - Mrs. Shagufta; Exam coordinator - Mrs. Afshana; and all the members of the management. Your guidance and encouragement have been invaluable to me. Without your support, I would not have reached this point in my life. I was about to give up, but you all were there for me when no one else was…

From the bottom of my heart, thank you so much. Your influence is something I will always carry with me, no matter where life takes me. You have all left an indelible mark on my heart; I am eternally thankful for that.

(Please read it in the same tune)

THANNKKKKKKK YOUUUUUUU TEACHERRRR !

DISCLAIMER

Before you embark on this literary journey, I feel it's my duty to give you a heads-up. This book isn't your typical read. It's more like having a witty friend by your side, always ready to hit you hard with truth and a smirk of humor. So, if you're ready to traverse the highs and lows of life's realities while laughing hysterically, buckle up your seatbelts! But fair warning, this isn't your grandma's bedtime story. It's a rollercoaster ride of emotions where humor meets honesty. For those brave enough to embrace the blend of reality and humor that awaits, consider this your invitation to join us on an adventure like no other. Let's dive in together and uncover the hidden treasures of wit, wisdom, and unfiltered honesty that lie ahead!

Dedication

To the misfits, the over-thinkers, and the perfectly imperfect souls—this is for you. For those who find humor in their stumbles and wear their quirks with pride, may you see yourself in these pages and know you're not alone. Here's to embracing our flaws, trusting the process, and laughing through the chaos of life together.

NOT A BIOGRAPHY - KNOW ME BETTER

Starting my second book feels a lot like taking another crack at mom's special recipe—hoping this batch turns out even better than the last. My debut book, 'Just a Flight Away,' was like my first attempt in the kitchen: a bit lopsided, a tad burnt, but made with love. Now, with 'Take Two: The Sequel,' I'm back at it with a pen instead of a mixing bowl, determined to cook up a story as satisfying as a warm slice of pie. It's been a journey of trial and error, mixing and tweaking, until I found just the right balance of ingredients. Along the way, I've learned that perfection isn't about flawless execution but embracing the messy, imperfect process of creation. So here's to second chances, learning from mistakes, and enjoying every delicious moment along the way.

ACKNOWLEDGEMENT

Firstly, to my Allah for providing the strength, guidance, and inspiration to bring this book to life. Without Your blessings, none of this would have been possible. To my family and friends, thank you for your unwavering support, laughter, and patience as I stumbled through the writing of this book. Your belief in me kept me going. From the books to grammars who helped spread the word and supported me along the way, your enthusiasm and encouragement have been incredibly uplifting. To my teachers, who imparted wisdom and guidance, and to everyone who helped me even a little bit, your contributions have been invaluable. And lastly, to myself. For pushing through the doubts, for finding the courage to keep going, and for believing in this journey even when it felt impossible. This book is a testament to the power of perseverance and self-belief. To every reader who picks up this book, thank you for embracing the journey of imperfection with me.

Acknowledgement

Your willingness to laugh at life's absurdities and find strength in vulnerability is what makes this endeavor truly worthwhile.

TABLE OF CONTENTS

Chapter 1. Believe In Yourself 1
- The Art of Ignoring Reality Checks 2
- Mishaps and Mirth.. 3
- Trust the Process 4
- Echoes of Believe 7
- Whispers of the Soul 9

Chapter 2. Perplexity and Personality: Navigating Life's Chaos 10
- The Power of Perplexity: Turning Confusion into Charisma 11
- Introverted Insights 13
- Extroverted Exuberance 15
- Soulful Serenade 17
- Whispers of the Soul 19

Chapter 3. Cracking the Mental Health Code 20
- Humor in the Depth of Depression 21
- Turning Struggle into Stand Up: Laughter as a Therapy. 24
- Relationship and Mental Health 26
- Rising above Darkness 28
- Whispers of the Soul 29

Table of Contents

Chapter 4. Techno Troubles 30
- Wild Web Whirlwind: Innocence Hijacked !!??? 31
- Social Media Circus: Highlights and Lowlights of Digital Life 33
- Swipe, Match, Deceive 36
- Deepfake Disasters: The Dark Side of AI Manipulation 40
- Digital Dilemmas 43
- Whispers of the Soul 45

Chapter 5. The Beauty Lies in the Eye Lens of the Beholder 46
- The Human Eye and the Rise Of Artificial Enhancements 47
- The Consequences of Chasing Perfection 49
- Embracing Natural Beauty in this Digital Age 50
- Beauty Beyond Pixels 52
- Whispers of the Soul 54

Chapter 6. Flourishing Humanity: Nurturing Seeds of Compassion 55
- Seeds of Compassion: Planting the Roots of Kindness 57
- Fostering Growth Through Appreciation 58
- Bridging Drives Through Understanding 59
- Compassionate Connections 61
- Whispers of the Soul 63

CHECK OUT MY PREVIOUS BOOK

 R_Diksha rated it ★★★★
Just now

 **Just a Flight Away**
by Farah Naaz

✓ Read

If you like short stories to read then this book is for you. It's a short story about a 20 year's old extrovert girl and a 23 year's old introvert guy who belongs to different countries. A really good short story about how they both get to know each other, become friends and then confess to each other, it's a story about long distance relationship. I liked the book, it was a good read, also as this is the first book written by Farah, there are some lackings(like it can be a little bit more detailed) but still I would recommend it to those who wants a quick read to lighten up their mood. This book showed us a process or we can say aspects? of relationship. The things everyone goes from once in their life while being in a relationship. And the teasing and roasting between both was really good 🌙💚

"Destiny is just like a director of a movie and you're the central character. You never know who the director will choose as your leading partner. Your part is just to play your roles efficiently."

Life is an iconic movie filled with mishaps and mirth, and you're the irreversible mishap, the blink-and-you'll-miss-it cameo that even the director regrets adding to the script.

CHAPTER 1

BELIEVE IN YOURSELF

*E*ver had one of those days where it feels like the universe is playing a cruel joke on you? You know, the kind of day where you've prepared for that dreaded math test like your life depends on it. You've sacrificed sleep, social outings, and even your sanity to memorize the quadratic formula and tackle those mind-numbing word problems about buying 200 bananas or calculating the speed of a train that nobody ever boards. I mean, who in their right mind needs to prove that a triangle is, in fact, a triangle? And don't get me started on the 200 bananas – who even has the fridge space for that many bananas? And why on earth should I care about the speed of a train when I've got a million other things to worry about? But alas, there you are, staring at the page in disbelief as your hopes of acing the test evaporate faster than an ice cube in a sauna. You've managed to fail at an Olympic level, and now you're left wondering how in the world you're going to explain this epic disaster to your parents without triggering a full-blown family meltdown. But fear not because, in times of crisis, there's always that one friend who swoops in with a piece of advice so profound. And what do they say? "Believe in yourself. You can do well the next time." Ah, yes, because apparently, confidence is the answer to all of life's multiple-choice questions. And you're well aware of how good you're at it. So, by now, I guess we all understand the importance of self-belief and why we SHOULD definitely believe in ourselves. So, let's dive deeper into it.

• The Art of Ignoring Reality Checks

Believing in yourself is akin to embarking on a journey in a world crowded with doubters and skeptics. It's like donning a cape and mask, ready to face the challenges that come your way. Yet, amidst the chaos and noise, there's a skill you must master – the art of ignoring reality checks. Imagine you're scaling the walls of doubt, only to have reality hurl stones of criticism at you. But instead of dodging, you stand tall, shielded by your unwavering self-belief. You see, believing in yourself isn't just about blind optimism; it's about acknowledging the obstacles while choosing to focus on the possibilities. It's about saying, "Yes, the odds may be against me, but I refuse to let them dictate my destiny." So, let's raise a toast to selective blindness, where we choose to see the world through the lens of our dreams rather than the lens of critics

- **Mishaps and Mirth**

The sweet symphony of self-doubt, playing on repeat like a broken record in the depths of your subconscious. Embracing inadequacy is not just a hobby; it's an art form. You're not perfect. You're far from it. But fear not, for mediocrity is your playground, and you're the reigning champion of stumbling through life like a newborn giraffe on roller skates. Imagine strutting through the halls of incompetence, your flaws shining like a beacon of averageness in a sea of overachievers. It's downright liberating to embrace your imperfections, to wear them proudly like a badge of honor that says, "I tried and failed spectacularly, but at least I tried." So go ahead, make mistakes with grace, stumble, and fall like it's an Olympic sport because, let's face It, nobody's watching anyway. And even if they were, they'd probably be too busy trying to stifle their laughter to offer any real help.

Revel in your own mediocrity, for in a world of flawless Instagram influencers and airbrushed magazine covers, being gloriously average is a rebellion in itself. So wear your flaws like a crown and remember: it's not about how many times you fall, but how many times you can turn it into a comeback and laugh at yourself before the world does it for you.

Oh! It was deep, though. I spent so long trying to find perfect words that sounded like this, and there are people like you who don't even post these texts on Instagram highlighting them. You better do it right now!

- **Trust the Process**

One of the most frequently used terms ever is "Trust the process." Ever heard of it? If you did, then you're probably one of those victims of social media who trust the process of waiting for your online persona to become your real personality, but sorry, filters can't fix personality flaws. "Trust the process" – those three magical words that promise enlightenment, success, or at least a decent outcome, all wrapped up in a neat little package of blind faith. It's like the IKEA instructions of life: confusing at first, but apparently leads to something resembling a functional piece of furniture.

Imagine you're baking a cake. You've got your ingredients laid out, your recipe in hand, and a hopeful heart full of dreams of a moist, delicious masterpiece. But then, disaster strikes – you accidentally swap the sugar for salt, the flour for powdered sugar, and throw in a dash of baking soda just for good measure. Panic sets in. Do you abandon ship? No! You take a deep breath, channel your inner chef, and whisper those magical words to yourself: "Trust the process." So, you shove that abomination into the oven, hoping against hope that somehow, someway, it will emerge as the glorious confectionery delight you envisioned. Spoiler alert: it doesn't. But at least you learned a valuable lesson about following recipes. Or perhaps you've just discovered that baking isn't your strong suit, and that's alright because not everyone deserves a sweet treat. Some, however, deserve a burnt one to complement their bitter personality. But definitely not you, my dear friend. You deserve the sweetest of all treats in order to counterbalance that bitterness within your soul.

Life is a lot like baking a cake – messy, unpredictable, and occasionally a complete disaster. But amidst the chaos, there's a glimmer of hope in those three little words: "trust the process." So, when life hands you lemons, sugar, and a questionable recipe, mix it all together and throw it in the oven with a hearty dose of faith. Who knows? Maybe you'll end up with a lemon meringue masterpiece or a hilarious Pinterest fail. Either way, embrace the process, laugh at the mishaps, and remember: even burnt cake can be sweet if you add enough frosting. Trust me; I'm a professional procrasti-baker.

Echoes of Believe

In the depths of doubt, where shadows loom,

Believe in yourself, and let your spirit bloom.

Trust in the process, though winds may sway,

For every mishap paves the path, come what may.

Through trials and tribulations, hold your ground,

Embrace the journey, and let hope resound.

In the tapestry of life, each thread holds worth,

For even mishaps can give way to mirth.

Humanize the depth of every emotion felt,

In the storm of uncertainty, let resilience melt.

With faith as your compass, navigate the tide,

Believe in yourself. Let your dreams collide.

In the symphony of existence, find your tune,

For every setback, a new dawn will soon.

So cherish the journey with every breath,

Believe in yourself, conquer life's depth.

Whispers of the Soul

Perfection is just a myth. You can never expect a person to be a perfectionist. Normalize people making mistakes, normalize people being clumsy. Making mistakes is not a crime, but owning up to them and taking responsibility is a mark of maturity and integrity. Instead of striving for perfection, we should embrace our imperfections. Our flaws and mistakes are what make us human, unique, and relatable. It's okay to be imperfect, to make mistakes, and to stumble along the way. By accepting our imperfections, we can free ourselves from the burden of unrealistic expectations and learn to love ourselves for who we are. In the end, we all are here for growth, and to achieve it, we should accept our flaws and those of others as growth is a beautiful journey of acceptance, persistence, and freelance, where you learn to enhance yourself with a balance in every circumstance. Believe in yourself, for your confidence is the seed that blossoms into trust from others. Trust in your own worth, and watch as the world aligns with the belief you hold within.

CHAPTER 2

PERPLEXITY AND PERSONALITY: NAVIGATING LIFE'S CHAOS

*I*ronically, this chapter is all about "Strength" and your "inner personality," but unfortunately, you have neither of them.... Anyways, coming back to the topic...

In life, we encounter two types of people: the catfish and the bad-bitch. The catfish are those who portray strength by acting aloof and, eventually, end up crying, seeking solace beneath the mask they're denying. On the flip side, the bad-bitch embraces their inner personality with a mix of raw emotions and unshakeable confidence, turning every challenge into a runway and every setback into a comeback. Isn't it weird seeing "emotions" and "confidence" in the same sentence? Well, that's what this chapter is all about—how emotions, confidence, strength, and our inner personalities intertwine to shape who we are.

• The Power of Perplexity: Turning Confusion into Charisma

You might have encountered perplexity in life, and magic begins when you turn the confusion into cha-rizz-ma. But let's address it; If you're reading this book instead of facing your problems, I can definitely guess your level of charismatic charm and your relationship status. Well, at least you have good taste in literature, even if your taste in humans is questionable.… **No offense, read the Disclaimer again**

Strength is the elusive trait that we all strive for yet often fail to grasp. It's like trying to hold onto a bar of soap in the shower—you think you've got it, but then it slips away, leaving you questioning your grip on reality. And let's be honest, your grip on reality isn't great, much like your hold on that relationship. In the end, what you're left with is just a guilt trip.

We often mistake stoicism for strength, but let's face it, suppressing emotions is like trying to contain a volcano with a tea strainer. Eventually, it's going to erupt.

"Strength" has no ideal definition. Being strong doesn't mean being powerful; strength isn't about dominance or emotionlessness; it's about resilience with empathy, empowerment without suppression, and impressiveness through authentic expression. Ever noticed how the funniest people are often the ones hiding the most pain? It's like they're wearing a mask made of laughter, hoping nobody sees the cracks underneath. But here's the kicker: humor isn't always a sign of happiness; sometimes, it's a coping mechanism, a shield against the harsh realities of life. So, the next time you meet someone who's always cracking jokes, don't just laugh along—ask them how they're really doing. Let's be real for a moment; life is messy, unpredictable, and downright confusing at times. But here's the silver lining: within that chaos lies the opportunity to discover your true self, embrace your quirks, and unleash your inner charisma. So, don't be afraid to get a little lost along the way. After all, it's in the darkest moments that we find our brightest light. So, let's raise a glass to the power of perplexity, where confusion meets charisma, and strength is found in the most unexpected places. Embrace your inner weirdo, laugh at life's absurdities, and remember, it's okay to be a beautiful mess. After all, in a world that's constantly changing, the only constant is the unpredictable nature of human existence. Talking about inner personality and unpredictable human nature, we know there are two types of inner personalities of a human: introvert and extrovert (yeah, I ignored ambiverts because those are like the middle child of personalities—constantly overshadowed and wondering where they fit in.

• Introverted Insights

First, let's illuminate the concept of strength, particularly in the realm of introverts. Strength for introverts isn't always loud or overt; it's often found in their ability to navigate the world with quiet resilience and unwavering determination. Despite misconceptions that introverts are shy or lacking in confidence, they possess an inner strength that runs deep. Introverts may not always flaunt their emotions or thoughts, but beneath their calm exteriors lies a world of complexity and depth. They are the silent guardians of society's sauciest secrets, their minds brimming with thoughts and musings that would even make the most outgoing extrovert blush. Introverts may not always share their innermost thoughts with the world, but within them, brews a storm of ideas and reflections waiting to be explored. Their introspective nature allows them to navigate life's challenges with grace and poise. But beneath their calm demeanor, introverts often harbor a secret: a mind teeming with thoughts and ideas that would surprise those who underestimate them. While they may appear innocent and unassuming on the surface, introverts possess a wit and wisdom that rivals even the most outgoing extrovert. Let's shed light on a lesser-known aspect of introverts: their surprisingly dirty minds. Despite their quiet demeanor, introverts often have a wicked sense of humor and a mind dirtier than extroverts. It's a well-kept secret that only those closest to them are privy to. While they may not broadcast their thoughts to the world, introverts have a knack for turning even the most innocent conversation into a risqué affair. So, to all the introverts out there: embrace your inner rebel, for your silent whispers hold more intrigue than the loudest shouts. And remember, while the world may underestimate your wild side, those who dare to dive deeper will uncover a world of hidden delights.

"Introverts are like the delicate petals of a flower, unfolding in the hushed embrace of dawn's first light. In the tranquility of their inner world, they find beauty in the subtle nuances of life, where silence speaks volumes and solitude becomes a canvas for self-expression. Like the flower, they bloom quietly, their essence radiating a unique and enchanting fragrance that captivates those who take the time to notice."

• Extroverted Exuberance

Now, let's dive deeper into the world of extroverts, those vibrant souls often mistaken for the cheekiest, naughtiest beings around. They're the life of the party, the ones who light up the room with their infectious energy and zest for life. But behind the laughter and the playful banter lies a depth of character that's often overlooked.

Extroverts are sometimes unfairly labeled as having the dirtiest minds, but there's more to them than meets the eye. While they may radiate confidence and charisma on the outside, they're also capable of introspection and thoughtfulness. It's just that their outgoing nature tends to overshadow these quieter moments, leaving their depth hidden beneath the surface. But let's not forget the vulnerable side of extroverts. When they shed a tear, it's often met with surprise and disbelief, as if their outgoing nature somehow shields them from feeling pain or sadness. But extroverts are human too, with emotions and feelings just like everyone else. They may be the life of the party, but they also experience the full range of human emotions, from joy to sorrow and everything in between. So here's to the extroverts for their ability to light up any room, their infectious laughter, and their knack for turning even the most mundane moments into unforgettable adventures. They may be the life of the party, but they're also the ones who remind us to embrace life's joys and face its challenges head-on, with a smile on our faces and a skip in our step.

"Just like a disco ball, extroverts shine brightest when they're surrounded by others. But even disco balls need a break to reflect on life's ups and downs because, let's face it, even the sparkliest souls have their dim moments."

Soulful Serenade

In the quiet of twilight, where shadows softly play,

Introverted whispers greet the end of the day.

In the midst of chaos, a moment to pause,

Where introverted introspection finds its cause.

With a wink to the stars and a nod to the moon,

Extroverted exuberance sings its tune.

A dance in the moonlight, a burst of cheer,

Bringing light to the darkness, drawing near.

In this delicate balance, where opposites meet,

Introverted depth and extroverted heat.

Like yin and yang, they intertwine,

Creating a symphony, both yours and mine.

So let's journey together through the depths of the soul,

Where introverted whispers and extroverted roll.

With humor as our compass

and meaning as our guide,

In this beautiful chaos, let our spirits abide.

Whispers of the Soul

Regardless of profession or personality, everyone harbors emotions. Just because someone is often seen laughing or telling jokes doesn't imply they lack feelings or can endure anything. Words and actions, no matter how small, can deeply affect people, regardless of whether they're introverted or extroverted. The distinction between strength and emotional detachment can be blurred. Strength isn't about dominance or being unfeeling; it's about resilience with empathy, empowerment without suppression, and impressiveness through authentic expression.

CHAPTER 3

CRACKING THE MENTAL HEALTH CODE

*W*elcome to the journey through the labyrinth of mental health, where every twist and turn reveals a new facet of our shared human experience. In this chapter, we'll navigate the complexities of the mind with empathy, understanding, and a touch of humor. Earlier, mental health was a topic veiled in mystery and stigma. It lurked in the shadows, a silent companion to our daily struggles, rarely acknowledged in polite conversation. Admitting to feelings of anxiety or depression was met with uncomfortable silence or whispered judgments, as if acknowledging our inner battles was a sign of weakness. But times are changing, and so too is our understanding of mental well-being. We now recognize that mental health is not a flaw but a fundamental aspect of our humanity. However, despite this progress, barriers still exist for those seeking help. The stigma surrounding therapy can cast doubt on the validity of our struggles and the legitimacy of our pain. But seeking help is an act of courage, not weakness. It takes strength to confront our inner demons and seek the support we need to overcome them. So, as we embark on this journey through the peaks and valleys of mental health, let's do so with open hearts and open minds. Let's embrace the humanity of our struggles, knowing that we are not alone in our journey. And let's remember that, even in our darkest moments, there is always hope for a brighter tomorrow.

• Humor in the Depth of Depression

Navigating the depths of depression feels like trying to climb out of a pit with greased walls. It's a silent struggle where even mundane tasks become monumental challenges. Think about canceling plans with friends, claiming a sudden "emergency," when in reality, you just can't face the world that day. It's oddly funny how we create elaborate excuses to hide our internal battles, presenting a facade of normalcy while feeling anything but normal. One particularly overlooked yet crucial topic is teenage depression. This is a time of emotional upheaval, where you've to keep up with societal and academic expectations, friendships are unstable, and the pressure to fit in is overwhelming. This is the time when they just begin to face the harsh reality of this world, but still, when they try to share it, they often hear dismissive remarks like, "What do you have to be depressed about?" As if the tumult of growing up isn't enough! Imagine a teenager skipping a social event, citing too much homework, when in truth, they're overwhelmed by anxiety and the fear of judgment. This age group often finds their feelings trivialized, adding to the weight they already carry. The rollercoaster of emotions, the struggle for identity, and the constant quest for acceptance make teenage depression a significant yet often ignored issue. Humor, in these moments, becomes a crucial lifeline. It's not about belittling the seriousness of depression but finding light amidst the darkness. Picture a teenager turning to their favorite comedy show after a tough day. Those moments of laughter provide a brief escape, a reminder that joy can still exist even in the toughest times. Humor bridges the gap between isolation and connection, making the weight of depression slightly more bearable. In the darkest moments, humor acts like a soothing balm for the wounded soul. It allows us to laugh at the absurdity of our situations, like when a teenager memes their own sadness or jokes about their overwhelming stress. These small bursts of humor are vital; they offer respite and build resilience. Even in the midst of profound struggle, a shared laugh can remind us that we're not alone in our battles and that hope and connection can be found in the most unexpected places. Navigating mental health stigma is akin to traversing a labyrinth of misunderstanding, where every step forward is met with skepticism and doubt. It's the struggle of confronting societal taboos and misconceptions surrounding mental well-being, where seeking help is often viewed as a weakness rather than an act of courage. Consider the scenario of a teenager grappling with anxiety and depression, silently yearning for therapy but unable to broach the subject with their family for fear of judgment. The mere mention of therapy is met with raised eyebrows and whispered gossip, perpetuating the stigma and shame associated with seeking help. Then there's the elusive concept of "mental health day," a day designated for prioritizing mental well-being that many are unaware of or dismiss as unnecessary. It's a reflection of society's reluctance to acknowledge the importance of mental health, relegating it to the sidelines while physical health takes center stage. But amidst the darkness, there is a glimmer of hope—a recognition that mental health is just as important as physical health. Imagine a world where mental health check-ins are as routine as annual physical exams, where seeking therapy is met with encouragement rather than judgment. It's a world where mental fitness training becomes a celebrated practice, akin to going to the gym to strengthen our bodies. In this world, self-care is prioritized, and seeking help is seen as a sign of strength, not weakness. This parallel world may seem like a figment of our imagination, but why not turn this vision into reality? It's up to us to challenge the stigma, normalize conversations about mental health, and create a world where seeking help is not only accepted but celebrated.

As we navigate the treacherous waters of mental health stigma, let us do so with empathy and resilience, knowing that every step forward, no matter how small, brings us closer to a world where seeking help is not only accepted but appreciated.

- **Turning Struggle into Stand Up: Laughter as a Therapy.**

Stand-up comedy isn't just about making people laugh; it's about turning pain into punchlines and transforming struggles into moments of triumph. Have you ever wondered why comedians often delve into their personal struggles on stage? It's because they know that laughter has a unique power to heal wounds that even the best medicine can't reach. Think about it: the people who fill the seats at comedy clubs, eagerly awaiting the next joke, are often the ones who have battled their own demons. They understand that laughter is more than just entertainment; it's a lifeline in a world that can sometimes feel overwhelmingly dark. For some, attending a therapy session might feel daunting due to societal judgment and stigma. In these cases, opting for a stand-up comedy show or watching comedy online becomes a therapeutic alternative. Even if just for a moment, they can escape reality and find solace in the laughter of others. For comedians, sharing their deepest struggles isn't just about getting a laugh; it's a form of therapy. It's a way to confront their pain head-on, to wrestle with their demons in the spotlight, and to emerge victorious on the other side. And for the audience, it's a reminder that no matter how difficult life may seem, there's always room for laughter and joy. In support groups and comedy clubs alike, laughter serves as a beacon of hope, a reminder that we're not alone in our struggles. It's a testament to the resilience of the human spirit, a light in the darkness that guides us through even the toughest times. So the next time life throws you a curveball, don't be afraid to find the humor in the situation. Embrace the absurdity, crack a joke, and watch as the weight of the world lifts from your shoulders. After all, laughter truly is the best medicine.

• Relationship and Mental Health

In the ever-evolving landscape of modern relationships, navigating the challenges of heartbreak and love is a journey that often intersects with the realm of mental health. As we traverse the winding paths of romantic entanglements and the dissolution of once-unbreakable friendships, we find ourselves confronted with the complexities of post-breakup mental health. The aftermath of heartbreak can leave us feeling adrift in a sea of emotions, grappling with feelings of loss, betrayal, and uncertainty. It's easy to become overwhelmed by the weight of our shattered expectations and bruised egos, wondering how we'll ever pick up the pieces and move forward. But amidst the wreckage lies a glimmer of hope – a reminder that healing is possible, even in the darkest of times. While casual dating may offer fleeting moments of pleasure, true fulfillment lies in the depths of genuine connection and mutual respect. It's a call to embrace vulnerability and authenticity, to approach relationships with open hearts and clear intentions.

So, how do we navigate the tumultuous waters of post-breakup mental health? It begins with self-care and self-compassion, acknowledging our emotions, and allowing ourselves the space to grieve. Seeking support from trusted friends, family members, or mental health professionals can provide invaluable guidance and perspective during this challenging time. Additionally, practicing mindfulness and engaging in activities that bring us joy can help to foster a sense of inner peace and resilience. Whether it's journaling, meditation, or spending time in nature, finding healthy outlets for our emotions can facilitate the healing process and promote emotional well-being.

Ultimately, the journey toward healing is unique to each individual, and there is no one-size-fits-all solution. But by honoring the sanctity of genuine connection and prioritizing our mental health, we can emerge from the ashes of heartbreak stronger, wiser, and more resilient than ever before.

Rising above Darkness

In the depths of the mind, where shadows dwell,

Cracking the mental health code is a tale to tell.

In-depth, the struggles we face,

Navigating the labyrinth of inner space.

In the silence of sorrow, depression's embrace,

A journey through darkness, seeking grace.

Yet amidst the turmoil, a light does shine,

Turning struggle into laughter, a therapy divine.

Through tears and laughter, we find our way,

In the intricate dance of night and day.

Relationships woven, hearts entwined,

A lifeline in the storm, a beacon defined.

So let's embrace the struggle with empathy's art,

Turning pain into purpose, healing each heart.

In the symphony of souls, let compassion reign,

Cracking the mental health code, we rise again.

Whispers of the Soul

In the mosaic of your struggles lies the canvas of resilience, each broken shard a tribute to your journey. Amidst the shadows, know that you're not alone; every trial is a brushstroke, painting the masterpiece of your soul. So, with courage as your compass, traverse the labyrinth of your mind. Seek, explore, and embrace the fragments of your being. For within the chaos lies the melody of your healing. Crack the code of your own mental health, and let the symphony of your strength guide you home.

CHAPTER 4

TECHNO TROUBLES

*W*elcome to "Techno Troubles," where we explore the hilariously frustrating world of modern technology. This isn't a deep dive into coding languages or tech specs—this is about the real-life, everyday chaos that technology brings into our lives. Remember the hype around digital currencies? We all thought we'd be millionaires by now, but instead, we're here checking our crypto wallets and wishing we could Delete our financial decisions. Techno trouble? Absolutely. Or what about the digital age robbing us of our innocence? Thanks to the internet, kids know more about "adulting" by the age of ten than we did at twenty. They won't buy the stork story; instead, they'll lecture you about DNA and genetic inheritance. Let's not forget about digital connections. Social media makes it easy to feel close to people, but those connections can be as fragile as your Wi-Fi signal during a storm. You think you've made a solid bond, but suddenly, you find out they're just as connected to someone else. It's like chemistry class all over again—you thought you had the perfect reaction, but it turns out they were busy forming compounds with someone else. And just like a failed experiment, you're left with nothing but a mess to clean up. The digital landscape is also rife with memes that capture our collective frustrations and joys. Memes have become our way of coping with the absurdities of tech life. They're the viral screenshots of our struggles, turning our techno troubles into shared laughs. While we laugh at these techno troubles, there's a meaningful side to our exploration, too. Technology has undeniably changed our lives—sometimes for better, sometimes for worse. By highlighting these humorous yet frustrating aspects, we aim to remind ourselves to strike a balance. Embrace the conveniences of technology, but don't let it control your life. After all, amidst the laughs and roasts, there's always a lesson to be learned about navigating this digital age with a sense of humor and a touch of wisdom.

- **Wild Web Whirlwind: Innocence Hijacked !!???**

Well, I guess you know what I'm talking about, right? That digital realm where you, once an innocent kid, stumbled upon things that made you question if the internet had an age restriction. Well, welcome to the club. Nowadays, kids are getting savvy, and by savvy, I mean they're finding out about stuff they have no business knowing at their age. Let's not kid ourselves; you did it too. Who better than you to understand the double-edged sword of the internet? Remember those innocent childhood questions that haunted you? The ones your parents answered with tales of storks and fairies? Yeah, the same parents who said a fairy dropped you gently on their lap. Well, let's set the record straight: fairies don't send little devils to parents. Your discovery of the internet quickly debunked those myths, right? With one click, you got answers to questions you didn't even know you had. The harsh reality of growing up in the digital age. Fast forward to today, where a child innocently searching for alphabet rhyme stumbles upon some unexpected online surprises. Meanwhile, parents are suddenly faced with explaining terms they never thought they'd have to discuss over dinner. The wonders of modern technology and parenting collide. These kids, they're digital sponges, absorbing every bit of slang, every meme, every viral video at an alarming rate. They mimic what they see, often without grasping the full context. And then they quote these gems in the most inappropriate places, like the classroom or, even worse, at family gatherings. You can't help but chuckle at the absurdity, but it's also a stark reminder of the wild world they're navigating, and just question yourself, "Who the hell taught this to them?" So, what's the takeaway from this digital whirlwind? The internet is an incredible resource, but it's also a bit of a minefield. As guardians of the next generation, it's crucial to guide kids through this maze. Teach them to find the gems while avoiding the pitfalls, and maybe share a laugh or two along the way.

- **Social Media Circus: Highlights and Lowlights of Digital Life**

We've all been there, Stuck in the digital race, scrolling through Instagram and falling for the façade of perfection plastered on every post. It's like we're trapped in a never-ending loop of FOMO (fear of missing out), where every highlight on their feed leaves us questioning highlights of our lives. You know those moments when someone posts a flawless selfie, meticulously edited to perfection, portraying an image of unattainable beauty standards. But then, in the next post or a glance at their previous feed, you catch a glimpse of their unfiltered reality—the imperfections, the flaws, the humanity that makes them real. It's as if we've become obsessed with projecting an image of flawlessness, striving to resemble a robot rather than embracing our true selves. But aren't our imperfections, our quirks, our unique flaws what make us human and differentiate us from mere robots? In the midst of this social media circus, let's not forget the beauty of being authentically imperfect, of embracing our humanity rather than striving for an unattainable digital perfection. It's like investing millions in what appears to be plastic, yet, with a silent pledge to protect the environment, you ingeniously choose to implant it within yourself, as if harboring the plastic's burden within, shielding the world from the pollution of perfection, one hidden alteration at a time. And let's not forget about filters. We've become experts at hiding behind digital masks, smoothing out our flaws, and erasing our imperfections with a swipe of the finger. But we have to face the fact that life isn't airbrushed. It's messy, chaotic, and downright unpredictable. So why do we insist on living in a digital fantasy world? Talking about the digital fantasy world, like online dating, we've amassed hundreds of friends online, but how many of them would show up if you needed a shoulder to cry on? It's like we've replaced genuine human connection with virtual likes and retweets, forgetting that real relationships require more than just a DM. If you viewed my story and yet did not wish me on my birthday, then you aren't my real buddy. By the way, your digital ex (if they existed) was once your friend online and then your boyfriend, so they must have wished you timely . Did it turn out real? Did it ever transition into genuine reality? That is exactly my point. I'm not saying you can't make genuine friends online, but you simply can't rely on them exclusively. It's essential to cultivate real-life connections, as they contribute significantly to your overall personality growth. Relying solely on digital media can ultimately detract from your character. Just look at how even extroverted individuals became introverted during the pandemic. So, let's not just acknowledge but actively prioritize genuine connections beyond the digital realm. Let's remember that behind every perfectly filtered post lies a real person with real struggles and insecurities. In the grand scheme of things, it's not the number of likes or the fleeting fame that truly matters—it's the authentic connections and moments of sincerity that give life its true meaning. Therefore, let's bid farewell to the filters and wholeheartedly embrace the messy, beautiful chaos of life. So celebrate the richness of authentic relationships and cherish the genuine moments that make life truly worthwhile.

- **Swipe, Match, Deceive**

Gone are the days of traditional arranged marriages, where couples met for the first time on their wedding day, bound to someone selected by their elders. But now, we're in a whole new era – the age of modern romance, or call it digital romance, to be fair. It's so modern that a mere swipe on our phone can bring us closer to the man or lady of our dreams, or at least, closer to our destiny. How sweet, right? It's ironic how we trust someone we've just swiped right on more than a friend we've known for years. Online dating promises connection and companionship, or so they say. So, you're probably on your phone, scrolling through profiles without a second thought, not bothering to put in any real effort. Talk about dedication! And if you end up with a dud of a partner, you blame it on fate, but if you luck out and find a gem, suddenly, it's all thanks to your stellar swiping skills. It's like we're playing a game of fate roulette, where we're too lazy to put in the effort to find a partner for a lifetime commitment. And as for that dream partner, you're fixated on, who knows who else they've swiped right on before you? Well, in that case, even you have been using it all wrong, such that your past swipe mishaps have landed you in the realm of dating apps and websites. From lovebombs to ghosting, it's a rollercoaster ride through the digital dating dictionary. You start off floating on cloud nine, basking in the warmth of affectionate texts and grand gestures. But just when you think you've found your happily ever after, reality comes crashing down in the form of ghosting. It's like dreaming of marrying your high school sweetheart only to wake up and realize you're chasing a celebrity crush. Ghosting isn't just about disappearing; it's about leaving you stranded in a sea of unanswered questions and unresolved feelings. You're left wondering if you should wait or move on, replaying every interaction in your head, trying to figure out what went wrong. Did you say something? Did you not say something? Was it your haircut? Or maybe it was the way you laughed at that terrible joke. Meanwhile, the ghost has moved on, probably using the same charm on another unsuspecting soul. Ghosting mostly happens when the ghost has gotten what they wanted – be it emotional validation, financial gain, or simply the thrill of the chase. They lose interest faster than you can say, "I thought we had something special." But losing feelings isn't like losing your keys; it's not something you can misplace and forget about. If they genuinely cared, they wouldn't vanish; they'd communicate. They'd have the decency to at least fake some courage instead of pulling a vanishing act. Communication takes effort and integrity, and that's the concept they've conveniently deleted from their dictionary, along with your self-respect. Coward ghost; the brave communicate. In the end, the ghosted grow stronger, while the ghosts remain forever haunted by their own spinelessness. Mostly, ghosting happens for one of three reasons: financial scams, losing feelings, or simply getting what they wanted from you. And let's be real. The "losing feelings" excuse is the ugliest of them all. I mean, come on, how do you lose feelings? It's not like misplacing your keys; you can't just forget where you left them. It's like saying you lost your book when the teacher asks you about your homework. It's just a pointless, feeble excuse for someone who couldn't be bothered to communicate like an adult. These are the folks who treat dating apps like a buffet, sampling a bit of everything without any intention of committing. The only thing they commit is a sin! They're the ones who line up dates back-to-back, ensuring they always have someone new to swipe right on. Casual romance has never been more casual – or more confusing. And those financial scams and identity theft. Some people actually create fake identities just to swindle unsuspecting victims out of their hard-earned cash. And why the hell are people falling for these scams? You literally check a hundred times before sending a 2 dollar transaction to your neighborhood shopkeeper, but you can't verify a real account on this app? It's mind-boggling! It really grinds my gears. So, next time you're tempted to swipe right, remember to guard your heart and your bank account. In the world of digital dating, not everything seems as it seems. Heartbreak in the age of connectivity is a special kind of torture. Rejection and betrayal online sting in ways our grandparents couldn't have imagined. You're constantly reminded of what you lost as their updates and posts pop up on your feed, each one a tiny dagger to the heart. It's like breaking up in front of an audience that cheers for your misery. The business of love has also never been more lucrative – for scammers, that is. Financial scams and romance frauds on dating apps are rampant. The sweet-talking charmer who seemed too good to be true often turns out to be just that – a scam artist looking to drain your bank account faster than you can say, "I think I'm in love, for sure… this time." Navigating the digital dating landscape requires a sturdy emotional shield. Emotional protection strategies become your trusty companions in this wild west of romance. Watch out for those who appear too perfect, too eager, or too interested in your financial affairs. Keep your senses sharp, trust your gut instincts, and remember: when it comes to online dating, it's always safer to swipe left on any red flags. Protecting your emotional well-being is paramount in this digital era. It's a veritable jungle out there, but with a blend of caution and humor, you can brave the hazards of modern dating without sacrificing your sanity, purity – or your heart.

Deepfake Disasters: The Dark Side of AI Manipulation

The marvels of modern technology! Once upon a time, our biggest tech worry was someone overhearing our phone conversations through a wiretap. But now? Now, we live in an age where a person's entire digital existence can be faked with frightening accuracy. Welcome to the era of deepfakes, where artificial intelligence is not just solving problems but also creating whole new sets of them. Deepfakes are like those obnoxious Photoshop fails on steroids, except they can talk, move, and, if done well enough, ruin lives. Imagine you wake up one day to find a video of yourself online, saying and doing things you'd never even dream of. Or maybe you did, but that's beside the point. It's the nightmare reality that many face nowadays. It's like playing the world's cruelest game of "Who Am I?" where everyone but you thinks they know the answer. And by listening to their answers, you've to google yourself and get the answer to "What the hell are they talking about ?" The tech wizards behind these digital fabrications are like puppeteers, pulling the strings of our online personas with the intent to deceive, defame, or just create chaos. And those cheap hackers. With just a bit or none of coding knowledge and a lack of conscience, these cybercriminals use AI to craft believable fake identities, crack into phones, and steal sensitive information. They're like digital pickpockets, but instead of your wallet, they're after your entire life. Imagine you're swiping through a dating app, thinking you've matched with a charming individual, only to realize later that you've been chatting with an Angel Priya (if you know, you know). You've basically fallen for a digital ghost, and there are thousands of identities and haunted lovers of them as well. Horrific, isn't it? What's worse is how this tech is weaponized for revenge or humiliation. Ex-partners, disgruntled colleagues, or just plain trolls use deepfakes to craft incriminating videos, spreading them far and wide. It's not just about ruining reputations; it's about wielding power. Nowadays, it's like, who needs to break someone's heart with mere words when they can destroy their life with a convincingly fake video? It's like giving a toddler a sledgehammer and watching the mayhem unfold. And yet, despite the havoc they wreak, deepfakes also serve as a grim reminder of our own gullibility. We scrutinize every Instagram post for filters and edits, yet we fall for these digital deceptions with alarming ease. It's as if the digital world has become an alternate reality where trust is the first casualty. You'd double-check the price tag before buying a pair of shoes, but somehow, a too-good-to-be-true video goes viral without a second thought. So, where do we draw the line? The reality is that technology itself isn't evil—it's the intent behind its use. In a world where we're constantly plugged in, the true danger lies in how we choose to wield these digital tools. As deepfake technology evolves, so must our skepticism and vigilance. We need to sharpen our critical thinking and remember that not everything we see is to be believed. The digital age demands a new level of awareness, where every click could be a trap, and every video could be a lie.

Digital Dilemmas

In the realm of the digital age, where innocence is hijacked,

A wild web whirlwind, where truth is often cracked.

Social media circus, with highlights and lowlights in tow,

Where the spotlight shines bright, but shadows also grow.

Swipe, match, deceive, a game of hearts and minds,

In the pursuit of connection, what truths do we find?

But beneath the surface lies a darker tide,

Where deepfake disasters thrive, in AI's deceptive stride.

Whispers of the soul lost in the digital noise,

Seeking solace amidst the chaos, amidst the ploys.

In this techno trouble, where innocence is at stake,

We navigate the maze, for truth's sake.

So let's heed the whispers amidst the digital roar,

Find strength in our souls as we strive for more.

In this chapter of techno troubles, let resilience be our guide,

For in the darkness, true humanity resides.

Whispers of the Soul

Technology brings countless benefits to humans, of which we are all aware, but discussing the drawbacks is much more important. Though I've used lighthearted humor here, these topics hold depth and are really something to rethink about. It's not the fault of the technology as it was discovered to solve the issues and make life easier, but those are humans who misuse it for their own selfishness. Technology, a mere tool, reflects humanity's boundless potential. Its true worth isn't in its capabilities alone but in the hands that mold it—may we wield it with wisdom, compassion, and an unwavering dedication to the common good, for therein lies our true progress.

CHAPTER 5

THE BEAUTY LIES IN THE EYE LENS OF THE BEHOLDER

*T*hey say beauty lies in the eyes of the beholder, and indeed, the human eye is a marvel of natural engineering, capable of feats that still baffle scientists and technologists. With an ability to perceive an astonishing range of colors, depths, and motions, the eye processes an immense amount of visual information in real time, something no camera can truly replicate. While a high-end camera might boast megapixels and zoom capabilities, it still falls short of the eye's seamless and dynamic focus, its intricate perception of light, and its natural depth of field. A camera needs a myriad of settings and adjustments to capture a moment perfectly, whereas your eye does this effortlessly, continuously adapting to changing light and focus without you even being aware of it. It's not just a window to the world but a window to the soul, reflecting emotions and thoughts in ways that no photograph can. Cameras may have their place, capturing and freezing moments in time, but the eye experiences these moments, giving them context and life. The comparison between the human eye and the camera underscores a deeper societal issue: our growing obsession with artificial enhancements. While cameras and photo-editing tools have their merits, they also promote a skewed perception of reality, pushing us towards an idealized and often unattainable standard of beauty. As we become more reliant on these technologies, we risk losing touch with the natural, unfiltered beauty that surrounds us—and that starts with the incredible, irreplaceable capabilities of our own eyes. Let's dive deeper into the topic.

• The Human Eye and the Rise Of Artificial Enhancements

The human eye stands as a testament to nature's unparalleled craftsmanship. Capable of perceiving millions of colors, adjusting to varying light conditions, and focusing on objects both near and far, the eye's capabilities surpass those of any camera lens. Cameras, despite their technological advancements, still struggle to capture the world with the same richness and accuracy. The eye's ability to perceive depth and motion in real time is something no camera can emulate perfectly. A camera needs a multitude of settings and manual adjustments to capture a single moment, while the eye does this seamlessly and continuously. The eye doesn't just see; it interprets, contextualizes, and adds emotional depth to every visual experience, making it far superior to any mechanical counterpart. In the quest for perfection, technology has given us tools to enhance, alter, and sometimes entirely fabricate our appearances. From the early days of black-and-white photography to today's high-definition, filter-laden social media posts, the evolution of camera technology has paralleled our growing obsession with artificial beauty. Modern cameras and editing software allow us to erase blemishes, smooth out skin tones, and even change physical features with just a few clicks. This digital enhancement has permeated our daily lives, especially through social media platforms where the pressure to present an idealized self is relentless. Filters can make our eyes bigger, our waists smaller, and our skin flawless, creating a digital version of ourselves that often feels more like a fantasy than reality. However, this pursuit of perfection comes at a cost. As we edit our photos to conform to these unrealistic standards, we inadvertently contribute to a culture that values appearances over authenticity. The irony is palpable: in trying to capture our best selves, we often end up masking our true selves. This constant comparison to digitally altered images can lead to feelings of inadequacy and a distorted sense of self-worth. The more we rely on these artificial enhancements, the more we risk losing sight of the natural beauty that is inherently ours. The rise of artificial enhancement highlights a critical need to balance technology with self-acceptance, reminding us that true beauty lies not in perfection but in authenticity.

• The Consequences of Chasing Perfection

The relentless pursuit of an idealized self-image, fueled by advanced camera technology and digital enhancements, has significant psychological and societal consequences. As individuals constantly compare themselves to meticulously curated and edited images, feelings of inadequacy and self-doubt proliferate. The societal pressure to appear flawless drives many to spend hours perfecting their digital personas, often leading to anxiety and depression. This obsession with perfection distorts our perception of reality, making it difficult to appreciate genuine, unaltered beauty. The irony is that while we strive to present our best selves online, we often end up feeling more disconnected from our true selves and from others. This quest for an unattainable standard of beauty creates a cycle of dissatisfaction, where the more we enhance our images, the less satisfied we become with our real-life appearances. The consequences extend beyond individual self-esteem, affecting how we perceive and value others, often reducing complex human beings to mere visual representations. In this digital age, it's crucial to recognize the pitfalls of chasing perfection and to cultivate a mindset that values authenticity and self-acceptance. Embracing our natural beauty and the unique imperfections that make us who we are is a radical act of self-love and resistance against a culture that profits from our insecurities.

- **Embracing Natural Beauty in this Digital Age**

In a world saturated with digitally enhanced images, a growing movement is pushing back, advocating for authenticity and the celebration of natural beauty. Embracing natural beauty in the digital age involves recognizing the value of our unique features and rejecting the unrealistic standards set by social media and photo-editing tools. Movements like the "no-filter" trend on Instagram and campaigns promoting body positivity are steps toward redefining beauty norms. But some bitches edit that "no filter look," add thousands of filters, re-edit it, save it, and then post it. What do you mean by pointing fingers at me? Well, I think we're off-topic, so let's continue. This no-filter (actual no-filter look) encourages us to show our real, unedited selves and to appreciate the diverse range of appearances that make us human. Practically, this means taking a step back from the constant urge to edit every photo and instead focusing on capturing moments as they are. It means celebrating the wrinkles, scars, and other features that tell our stories rather than hiding them. By doing so, we not only foster a healthier self-image but also contribute to a culture that values authenticity over artificial perfection. Embracing natural beauty is about more than just appearances; it's about fostering a deeper connection with ourselves and with others, grounded in reality and genuine appreciation. In navigating the digital landscape, let us remember that true beauty is not about meeting an ideal standard but about embracing the uniqueness that each of us brings to the world. Maturity is when you realize that those minor imperfections truly enhance your beauty. Those freckles, Those birthmarks, those acne marks, etc. These are not imperfections, but for some, They are. Ever imagined why people fear acne marks but love dimples, freckles, etc? Why are these not treated as a flaw? Why are these faked if they don't have it naturally? It's just a human tendency. The rise of high beauty standards. It's just how the Human brain works. They fix a certain standard, and if you don't fit in there, then you're just treated as an alien. The exploration of beauty through the lens of technology and nature reveals much about our values and priorities. As we navigate the digital age, it's important to remember that technology is but a tool—a reflection of humanity's potential. Its true measure lies not in its capabilities but in the hands that guide it. Let us wield it with wisdom, compassion, and a steadfast commitment to the greater good, always remembering that true beauty lies in authenticity, not perfection.

Beauty Beyond Pixels

From a fervent faith to a skeptic gaze,

Human beings are trapped in a hypocritic maze

They preach self-love with rise and grace

One dark spot, and it's hard to embrace!!

An unflattering pic and the confidence erase

Leads to tabs and searches to eliminate in different ways

The camera lens displays the beauty and grace

One beauty-marketing and the APPLE of the eye pays

The craters of the moon don't conceal the beauty it displays

What makes you think the scars on your face will showcase?

Beauty isn't perfection

Perfection doesn't mean beauty …. As at the end…

The behavior and personality are what which remain.

Whispers of the Soul

In the labyrinth of existence, true beauty is not found in the polished façade but in the raw, unfiltered essence of our souls. As we traverse the digital expanse, let us not merely navigate but cultivate gardens of authenticity, where each bloom bears the imprint of our vulnerabilities and triumphs. For it is in the tangled vines of imperfection that the most exquisite roses of humanity unfurl, reminding us that true beauty lies not in flawlessness but in the courage to embrace our authentic selves. In this journey called life, may we cherish the wildflowers of our uniqueness, for they are the vibrant hues that paint the canvas of our shared humanity with boundless richness and depth. And in the quiet whispers of our souls, let us remember: "In the garden of authenticity, the most beautiful flowers bloom from the seeds of imperfection." Just like the resilient lotus, which rises from the murky depths, its pristine petals untouched by the surrounding mire, so too does our authenticity emerge from the challenges and imperfections of our lives, shining brightly amidst the darkness.

CHAPTER 6

FLOURISHING HUMANITY: NURTURING SEEDS OF COMPASSION

*I*t's truly ironic how, in a world that often preaches positivity and kindness, the pillars of humanity seem to crumble beneath the weight of conflict, injustice, and indifference. The essence of kindness, once considered a cornerstone of human interaction, appears to have faded into the background amidst the chaos of modern life. We witness atrocities like the ongoing violence in Palestine, where innocent lives are lost every day, yet the world remains largely silent, complicit in its inaction. It's a stark reminder of the disconnect between our words and our actions, between the values we espouse and the reality we inhabit. The plight of Palestine serves as a poignant example of the urgent need to rekindle the spirit of kindness and compassion within our global community. In the face of unimaginable adversity, the Palestinian people have shown incredible resilience and compassion, refusing to be silenced or broken by oppression. As they continue to endure the injustices inflicted upon them, it is incumbent upon us as global citizens to stand in solidarity with Palestine, to amplify their voices, and to advocate for their rights to freedom, justice, and dignity. By supporting Palestine, we not only uphold the principles of justice and human rights but also reaffirm our commitment to kindness, empathy, and compassion for all people. Together, let us work towards a future where the voices of the oppressed are heard, where justice prevails, and where kindness triumphs over adversity. In times of crisis and adversity, it becomes increasingly evident that kindness is not just a fleeting sentiment but a profound and enduring force for good. It transcends boundaries of race, religion, and nationality, offering solace, hope, and healing to those in need. Yet, kindness is not solely reserved for grand gestures or acts of charity. It exists in the small, seemingly insignificant moments of our daily lives—the smile shared with a stranger, the hand extended in friendship, the words of encouragement offered in times of doubt.

These gestures, though small in scale, possess the power to uplift spirits, forge connections, and transform lives in ways we may never fully comprehend.

It's often said that people won't remember what you gave them, but they will always remember how you made them feel. In the tapestry of human experience, it's the threads of kindness that weave the most enduring and meaningful patterns. It's a reminder that in a world fraught with division and discord, our capacity for empathy and compassion remains our greatest asset. As we navigate the complexities of our shared existence, let us not underestimate the significance of our small acts of kindness. Let us strive to cultivate a culture of compassion where every interaction is imbued with empathy, understanding, and respect. And let us never forget the profound impact that even the smallest gestures of kindness can have on the lives of those around us.

- **Seeds of Compassion: Planting the Roots of Kindness**

Ever noticed how empathy is like Wi-Fi? You can't see the thin connection, but you definitely know when it's not there! It's the unsung hero of human connection. The act of sowing seeds of empathy is basically becoming the

Sherlock of emotions—detecting those subtle vibes and responding with a compassionate high-five or a virtual hug. In a world full of speakers, being an empathetic listener is a rare gem. So next time someone rants about their latest mishaps, remember, you're not just hearing their words; you're planting seeds of empathy. It's like tending to a garden of feelings, where every color of the flower leaves a sense of comfort and understood feeling, not overlooked. And speaking of kindness, it's not just about writing big checks or rescuing kittens from trees. It's the little things, like holding the elevator door for the other person or just talking to someone politely with a smile on your face (not for so long that the other person starts referring to you as a creep). So let's celebrate the unsung heroes of kindness—the ones who refill the office coffee pot without being asked and patiently listen to their friend's betrayal stories for the millionth time. Because in a world where you can be anything, why not be someone's reason to smile?

• Fostering Growth Through Appreciation

Appreciating people for their minor improvements and efforts brings a lot of difference to their growth and ours. You know those people who always have a compliment ready, like they're handing out free samples of happiness?

Yeah, they're the real MVPs of kindness. Just like how a minor mishap can turn you off in such a way, a minor appreciation can be the highlight of their day. It's the little things that water the garden of goodness. But let's get real for a second. Kindness isn't always rainbows and butterflies. Sometimes, it's biting your tongue just to bring a smile to the other's face so that they don't get hurt by our words. Well, I know it's not easy, but when everyone in this world is busy being savage, sassy, disrespectful, and cool, be different and win hearts by being generous and kind. People may forget the sassy rich person, but what they'll always remember is your behavior, nature, and personality. It's about choosing compassion over cynicism, even when the world feels like a dumpster fire. So here's to the unnoticed heroes of kindness—the ones who choose to sprinkle a little extra love in a world that could use a refill. Because in the grand symphony of life, kindness is the melody that makes it all worth dancing to.

- **Bridging Drives Through Understanding**

Amidst the chaos of contemporary existence, cultivating connection becomes an art form, a delicate ballet of hearts seeking solace in each other's embrace. Constructing bridges of understanding demands we embrace vulnerability and courage, stepping beyond our comfort zones to engage with those whose experiences may differ from our own. In shared moments of laughter and tears, we find common ground, dispelling misconceptions and nurturing a sense of belonging that transcends boundaries. Through open-mindedness and active listening, we create spaces for dialogue and collaboration, laying the foundation for a more inclusive and compassionate society. As I navigate life's labyrinth, I find myself drawn to the allure of trendy shoes, not merely for their fashion statement but for the symbolism they hold. Like ever-evolving trends, empathy adapts, molding itself to the shifting landscape of human experience. With each step forward guided by kindness and understanding, we leave imprints of compassion on the sands of time. Each footfall is a testament to empathy's power, a beacon of hope illuminating the path toward a brighter, more interconnected world.

Compassionate Connections

In the garden of humanity, seeds of compassion sow,

Planting roots of kindness, watch them grow.

Fostering growth through appreciation's embrace,

Bridging divides with understanding's grace.

In a world often divided, where differences collide,

Nurturing empathy, let compassion be our guide.

For in the heart of understanding, true unity lies,

Blossoming humanity under open skies.

So let's tend to the garden with care and devotion,

Watered by empathy, each heartfelt emotion.

In the flourishing of compassion, let's take our stand,

For it's through love and kindness we truly expand.

Whispers of the Soul

In the symphony of life, let empathy be your melody, weaving harmonies of kindness and understanding wherever you go. Shine bright, knowing that while some may cast shadows, your light illuminates paths of compassion, regardless of what may come your way. Walk with grace, for in the dance of empathy, every step is a testament to the beauty of humanity, even when met with discordant notes. Embrace the journey, knowing that in nurturing empathy, you sow seeds of love that bloom in the hearts of others, even amidst thorns of adversity. So, let your empathy be a beacon of hope, a guiding star in a sky of uncertainty, for in the end; it's not about expecting the same in return but about being true to the melody of your soul as you have more influential power than the celebrity as people are in touch with you, you can inspire them to be kind and generous.

Thank you for taking the time to read my book. I hope it resonated with you despite any shortcomings it may have had. Your feedback is incredibly valuable to me, as it motivates and encourages me to improve and continue writing. If you haven't already, I would greatly appreciate it if you could leave a review on platforms like Amazon or Instagram. Your support means the world to me. Also, don't forget to scan the QR code at the back of the book for additional content , you can also scan the QR code below to share your reviews

Thanks and Regards
Lots of love

Farah Naaz

www.ingramcontent.com/pod-product-compliance
Lightning Source LLC
LaVergne TN
LVHW041543070526
838199LV00046B/1816